Soul You Vol. I

THE GRAND AWAKENING

Soul You Vol. I: The Grand Awakening. Copyright 2021 by Sherika Frazier Duncan. All rights reserved. No part of this publication may be reproduced, distributed, or transmitted in any form or by any means, including photocopying, recording, or other electronic or mechanical methods, without the prior written permission of the publisher, except in the case of brief quotations embodied in critical reviews and certain other noncommercial uses permitted by copyright law. For permission requests, write to the publisher, addressed "Attention: Permissions Coordinator," 3819 Ulmer Court, Tallahassee, FL 32311.

Sherika Duncan books may be purchased for educational, business or sales promotional use. For information, please email the Sales Department at sales@sherikaduncan.com.

First Edition Printed, February 2021
Library of Congress Cataloging-in-Publication Data has been applied for.
ISBN: 978-1-7364355-0-2

Table of Contents

AWAKENING 1

EGO 2

ENERGIES 4

    PLANETARY ENERGY 4

    ASTROPHYSICS 6

    ENERGY SOURCES 8

    SEVEN CHAKRAS 11

    SOUND THERAPY 12

    ANCIENT EGYPT 13

    ANKH 15

    KUNDALINI ENERGY 16

    KINETIC ENERGY 18

    LOWER FREQUENCY HABITS: 19

SPIRIT 21

    SOUL 22

    GUT 26

OMNIPRESENCE	27
MELANIN	30
REALITY	34
TIME	35
HOLIDAYS	36
THE ARRIVAL	37
BELONGING	38

Disclaimer of religion: the views or opinions expressed in this book are those of the author and don't necessarily reflect the official policy of position of any religious affiliation.

Awakening

If we knew our expiration date, what would we do differently?

Ever asked where people originated from?
What about the whole planet?
The atmosphere and the galaxies?
Or even the ocean?

The thoughts of what we were doing before entering this world in physical form intermittently run through our minds. A woman is a portal to the universe and a divine being. We are immortal, eternal spirits; whatever we do presently repeat into eternity. Frequency is like attraction. What you attract will attract back to you. If you desire and long for positive energies, it will come to you, and if you want corrupt energies, those energies will attract you.

Divine feminine represents the link to the piece of our consciousness responsible for nurture, intuition, and compassion, despite our gender—creation, feeling, population, love, and collaboration.

Divine masculine embraces competition enjoys conquering, continually scanning for the next new challenge.

Divine feminine and masculine energy notes: *there exists a divine balance of masculine and feminine principles.*

Ego

The Ego introduces insecurities, mental, behavioral habits, trigger details of prior occurrences, and the necessity to remain precise. The conceited character, such as self-protection, can be somewhat toxic and untamed.

Silence can train our minds to tune out the noise to seek inner peace. Feelings are essential to us. We must learn how to understand our feelings and evaluate how certain emotions are invoked. Most of us just want to have our Ego stroked. Learning how to grow by talking about our struggles and learning experiences is challenging. It usually is uncomfortable when we check ourselves.

Awakening Notes: *Hurt people hurt people*

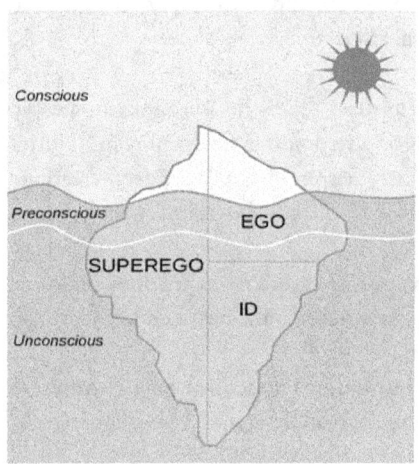

This Photo by Unknown Author is licensed under CC

Notes

_____

_____

_____

_____

_____

_____

_____

_____

_____

ENERGIES

PLANETARY ENERGY

Jupiter is the sign of prosperity, future, and growth.

Saturn is the sign of karma and profession.

Mars supplies us the energy to be active and not idle.

Moon signifies our understanding and attachment.

There are two groups of planets, which are the inner and outer planets. Inner planets include the Sun, Moon, Mercury, Venus, and Mars. The outer planets act even more slowly because they influence more significant trends in our life.

This Photo by Unknown Author is licensed under CC BY-SA

Equinox is when the Earth's axis tilts neither towards nor away from the Sun two times a year. Equinox is a combo of two Latin words. Aequus refer to equal-nox, which means night. An equalization of hours in a day causes a bending of the light's rays primarily responsible for the Sun appearing above the horizon when the Sun's position is below the horizon.

In the Northern Hemisphere, the Vernal Equinox falls around **March 20th or 21st**. As opposed to the Southern Hemisphere, the Sun moves south across the celestial equator on or about **September 22nd or 23rd**.

During this timeframe, the days become longer and cause the Sun to rise and set. A solstice occurs throughout the Earth's axis leans towards the Sun at its maximum potential. The Sun rises at noontime. It's the highest altitude that varies, so limited for some days before and following the summer solstice.

Planetary Energy Takeaway: *The Sun heats our oceans, awakens our climate, creates our weather patterns, and supplies power. The Equinox and solstice are significant calendar periods that arrive by the Sun's location and connect to the seasons.*

ASTROPHYSICS

Astrophysics is the part of astronomy focused on the real nature of stars and various celestial bodies, including regulations and physics principles with the understanding of astronomical observations.

Stars are from hydrogen clouds of dust called a stellar nebula. Over millions of years, the temperature rises to millions of degrees to form a **protostar**.

Isn't it mindboggling when we die, we typically return to dust buried in the sand?

Nebula star (white dwarf - beginning) Massive main-sequence star(adult) transition into four different patterns, such as:

Red supergiant stars (Hydrogen, Helium, Carbon, Oxygen, Neon, Magnesium Silicon, and Iron) explodes into the Supernova is heat and light energy that outshine all other stars. Temperatures become so hot it explodes into *stardust*.

Two types: Neutron star made of neutrons electron forced merged protons

Astrophysics Takeaway: *We are all derived from stardust.*

This Photo by Unknown Author is licensed under CC BY-

ENERGY SOURCES

There are two different frequency types synthetic and cosmic.

Cosmic frequencies- There are various magnetic field strengths in our solar system.

Blackhole intense gravity light can't escape nearby objects such as stars. Global warming is human-induced warming of the Earth system.

This Photo by Unknown Author is licensed under CC BY-

A **Magnetosphere** is the Sun's gigantic area of magnetism enveloping our planet and protecting us from the fury of the Sun. It deflects most solar material sweeping towards us from our star at 1 million miles per hour or more.

The Sun sends us magnetic fields paired with abundant amounts of information being sent to its *Sun people*. When we have an increase in melanin, we are resonating at a higher frequency capacity—the practice of Sun-gazing and grounding the act of putting our feet in the grass. We are charging up as a light show. We become aligned with cosmic download;

Is everything a vibration?

The frequency creates an attraction, drawing something into our atmosphere because we are making our own destruction. As we are being connected, the Sun-affects us through the disruptive planets; the Moon, Sun, and planets aligned together to stay balanced. Sunlight is scattered and filtered through Earth's atmosphere and is obvious as daylight when the Sun is above the horizon. We, hue-man, maintain our unique electromagnetic field. Natural resources of crystals and matter are *amethyst, lapis lazuli, blue or purple sapphire, purple violet tourmaline, or rhodonite.*

Do we know where we are headed?
Are we departmentalizing what is happening?

Planetary Energy Notes: Every human body cell *has its own electromagnetic field.*

Notes

_____

_____

_____

_____

_____

_____

_____

_____

_____

_____

SEVEN CHAKRAS

Ancient wisdom about the seven chakras for consciousness healing is considered vibrational frequencies in specific seven sections of the body.

Name	Location	Reference
Root Chakra	Found centered at the base of the spine and tailbone.	Survival, Being, Grounded, Family
Sacral Chakra	Found centered lower abdomen below navel	Creativity, Sexuality, Pleasure
Solar Plexus Chakra	Found centered above the navel	Will Power, Self-Esteem
Heart Chakra	Found centered above the heart	Love, Compassion, Inner Peace, Joy
Throat Chakra	Found centered of the throat	Communication
Third Eye Chakra	Found centered on forehead between eyebrows	Intuition, Wisdom, Imagination
Crown Chakra	Found centered of the highest point of head	Spirituality

Chakra Takeaway: Our food choices are incredibly crucial for chakra alignment.

Balance Masculine and feminine
Understanding the frequency and vibration
Higher dimensional force
No shape or form, no time
Within and without dimension in a state of feeling
Fifth-dimensional awareness

SOUND THERAPY

We are naturally connected to all types of vibration and frequency, good or bad. The healing frequency of 528 Hz healing frequency has been investigated and examined by biogenetic biochemists sampling it in their labs to restore DNA damage. There are two different frequency types synthetic and cosmic. **Cosmic frequencies**- there are various magnetic field strengths in our solar system.

It is the harmonic vibration that lifts our hearts and divine voice in harmony with heaven. The frequency can boost our immunity 100% by sparking antioxidant activity. 528 Hz waves also guard the central nervous system of alcoholics by an estimate of 20%.

Music is a powerful sound - recognize fast and associate it immediately 50-90 beats per heart rate dis-synchronize beats are off rhythm. **Classical music** certain tones to stimulate a high brain function If we've ever attended a sound bath, we know about the healing power of sound. Singing bowl will sing by rubbing. The **Singing bowl** sounds will help clarify and promote relaxation.

ANCIENT EGYPT

The Ancient Egyptian civilization possessed longevity, stability, and divine balance with Great Pyramids, royal monuments. Hermeticism is based on Hermes' writings famously known for multiple Emerald Tablets written by Thoth the Atlantean. Thoth the Atlantean was also historically evidently known as being influential to human development. Many Egyptian statues exist today with apparent African facial features damaged due to chiseled noses to cowardly cover the truth of their race.

Immortality

There exists preserved Ancient Egyptian funerary text within Egyptian signs depicting Pharaohs' possessed wisdom on how to beat death by transitioning into immortal through cross-range chemical pathways of crystallized state of living in the Quantum Domain inscribed on pyramids and coffins.

This Photo by Unknown Author is licensed under CC BY-SA

ANKH

The ankh or key of life is an ancient Egyptian hieroglyphic symbol that was most used in writing and in Egyptian art to represent the word for "life" and, by extension, as a symbol of life itself. The ankh represents an ancient Egyptian hieroglyphic symbol that means a key to life. Egyptians used it frequently in their writing and in Egyptian drawings to describe the concept of "life" and, in addition, as a representation of life. The ankh has a teardrop-shaped oval circle cross form in the upper strip.

Ancient Egypt Takeaway: *This is chronologically documented by our original ancestors, the Egyptian people.*

KUNDALINI ENERGY

Kundalini is a system of meditation directed toward the release of kundalini energy.

Mediation allows us to step outside of time. The right people influence the human body by allowing our blood to flow and more alive; plasma good and healthy for our energy;

This Photo by Unknown Author is licensed under CC BY-NC

Notes

KINETIC ENERGY

Scientists believe that almost all your body's mass comes from the quarks' kinetic energy and the gluons binding energy.

Are we all just energy?

Kinetic Notes: *We are living in an ocean of vibrational energy.*

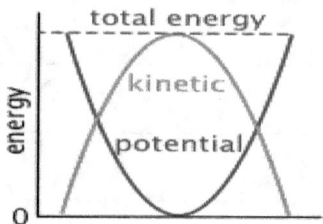

[This Photo](#) by Unknown Author is licensed under [CC BY-SA](#)

LOWER FREQUENCY HABITS:

Levels of the spectrum through multiple senses such as sight, hear, touch, smell. News media, public, radio low vibrational music. Junk food and processed food are the first things to remove from our life if we are looking to improve our frequency. Nutrient deficient foods provide nothing, but they slow us down and increase our organs' strain.

Eat high-vibe foods.

This Photo by Unknown Author is licensed under CC BY-

Toxins

Various products, environments, cosmetics, cleaners, and pollution sources lower our frequency. Once our body become ill it is impossible to develop a higher frequency. We should remove all harmful toxins from our lives.

Release toxic environments.

Consistent Exposure to Electronics

Electronic devices interfere with our energy and cause it to drain down by keeping it close by for longer periods.

It is essential to clear stress, anxiety, anger, guilt, or resentment. *Limit watching Tell-lie-vision.*

What is the source of prana?

There are three principal sources of prana: the air, from which we get air prana; the earth, from which we get ground prana; and the Sun, from which we get solar prana.
Energy.

Electricity

Electricity is everywhere, even in the human body. Our cells are specialized to conduct electrical currents. Electricity is required for the nervous system to send signals throughout the body and to the brain, making it possible for us to move, think, and feel.

Lower Frequency Takeaway: A disruption in electrical currents can lead to illness. Listen to higher vibrational music like 432 Hz. Your story is worth history.

SPIRIT

We are hue-man who possesses a divine light.

Did we behave in a manner that take us one step closer to our higher self?
Or did we behave one step closer to a harsh environment?
Or were we stagnate?

We are responsible for the way for which we live.

What do we choose, heaven or hell?

Level: Spirit

There are unlimited possibilities of frequencies that exist outside of time. Our spirit attaches or rejects to blend us with the creator.

Spirit Takeaway: *We are far beyond what meets the eyes!*

SOUL

What do we need to live for?
When we die, what will be the most highlighted
moments in our life mentioned?

Our soul is an instrument that must be tuned to express the right frequency. We must take care of ourselves and stay consciously aware. When we experience a cardiac arrest, it is usually the results from an electrical disturbance in the heart. Although, it is not the same as a heart attack because the main condition is loss of consciousness and unresponsiveness.

What effects does our intention cause?

Everything we do is a building block for the next step we take. Be mindful of what righteous or evil seeds we are planting in our gardens. The soul helps hue-man to find truth and understanding of our true soul role purpose.

A soul can either be mortal or immortal. The body's purpose is to experience the assignment of that life. Our souls are here on assignment, so it does not rely on the body. The soul exists without a body because when our body vanishes, the soul will not be destroyed in any natural process because it is invisible.

Soul Takeaway: *There can only be one personified essence of us. Colloidal gold has amplified electricity in the highest electromagnetic field. Egyptians wore chains and drank gold because of frequencies. Our physical, immune, and mental strength is our true health. It is vital to create an environment to maintain the natural alignment of ascension. Otherwise we are descending.*

Notes

_____
_____
_____
_____
_____
_____
_____
_____
_____
_____

Teach me because it genuinely can grow me!

Pineal gland

Knowledge resides in people's minds in two forms: tacit and explicit. And while explicit knowledge can readily be captured and shared, tacit knowledge in the form of beliefs, insights, experience, and know-how may be challenging to report and express.

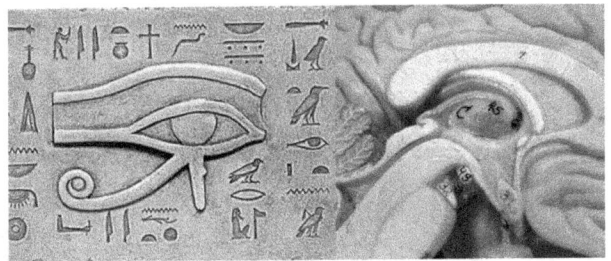

This Photo by Unknown Author is licensed under CC BY-ND

GUT

Trust your gut

The ***heart*** is the first organ to form as the faint heartbeat becomes intense as the nervous system is developed. Other organs begin to grow as our heart transfers nutrients. Individuals with low vagal tone index experience depression, heart attacks, loneliness, negative feelings, and stroke.

Here's a List to Restore Vagal Tone
Take a cold shower in the morning.
Sing, laugh, hug
Probiotics
Alter heart rate variability
Reduce jaw tension.
Fast intermittently Learn to love cold temperatures Adjusting to temperatures colder than average body temperature.
Meditate daily Practice Tai Chi Have massages often Neck and foot massages
Sleep on the right side Lying on the back
sleeping on the right
electrical waves synced with music.
Supplement zinc and serotonin (5-HTP)

Zinc is crucial to Vagus Nerve function. Optimal Vagus Nerve function, associated with strong social connections, positive emotions, and better physical health.

OMNIPRESENCE

Our Creator made this universe with unlimited God frequencies of vast energies.

How can the same Creator of this world come from the same place made for us?

How does the cosmos interact with us? Is it in rhythm with the planet?

We are all fragmented energies from different clusters of electrons. Yet, we are all a part of the same energy source. The sheer power that is not created or destroyed. Surely there must be a unique supernatural sacred place of God, divine, deities, souls, spirits, or ghosts. Everything is not to be naturally explained scientifically.

Our Creator is supernaturally out of this world!

There exists a lightness in embracing the universe through infinite spaces where higher consciousness concurrently flows as frequency. The cosmos contributes gifts that penetrate our consciousness. Since energy is within everything.

What exactly is it?

Energy can be thermal, radiant, chemical, nuclear, electrical, motion, sound, elastic, and gravitational. The electromagnetic charge of a force field in various positions in space exists inside the omnipresent universe. *Energy is categorized by kinetic and potential transfers to each other.* (Genesis 1:1-31) They work in harmony to acknowledge their position and then move in any direction. Sometimes friction will occur that creates an imbalance to correct itself higher or lower energy shifts around to work in harmony. The two higher or lower energy shifts working together can change the climate.

How many of us are longing to restore ourselves to full energy?

Kinetic energy is the act of a moving object in motion in any direction like running water. **Potential energy** is the position of a thing like the peak of a tall ocean wave.

Let us be like water!

This Photo by Unknown Author is licensed under CC BY-SA

(2 Peter 3:5)

Whisper brain waves triggering electrical signals of receiving vibrations of awareness, such as an urge to trust our intuition inside our gut. Shift the energy to become lighter from heavy by removing the roadblocks in our way.

Omnipresence Takeaway: *We are not by happenstance!*
(collective consciousness to derive; what we believe)

MELANIN

From roughly 1.2 million through less than 100,000 years ago, archaic humans and homo sapiens were dark-skinned. Melanin is a dark natural pigment (biochrome) found in cosmos, water, land, skin, hair, feathers, scales, eyes, and some internal membranes. It is dynamic in every aspect of the cell in the core of the human being and the human being's surface. Every part of the nervous system has many black dots through it, and these Black dots carry information. Our bodies are a communication system. Everything is connected to everything else. It works through all living beings as light particles called biophoton, which is subtle energy carrier cells have connections to other cells called interneurons electrons, and light flows between cells. It is a supercomputer. A study Energy is directly absorbing from the melanin in your skin and transform into energy in our bodies. A master molecule that steers how the body communicates.

Darker skin holds a concentrated type of melanin called eumelanin, which act as a natural ozone layer. melanin is photo-protective against UV rays prevents fast-paced aging; This Melanin is produced by so-called melanocytes in the skin. Melanin is the body's own way to protect the skin against Sunlight.

Skin Care

Melanin skin pigmented people possess dark hair, skin, and eyes. It helps protect our skin from UV rays. We have the lowest ceramide content. Ceramides are a crucial component of our skin's barrier that locks in moisture. The Sun people have low ceramide levels result in more water loss and dry, flaky skin.

Oily skin

So, having oily, acne-prone skin in some areas and dry skin in other regions washing daily with the *glycolic (AHA)* or *salicylic (BHA)* cleanser will reduce fine lines' appearance, uneven pigmentation, and acne.

Oily and Acne

It is essential to use an *oil-free* or *non-comedogenic* moisturizer and leave pores to unclog. Melanin dry skin Sun people should use a moisturizer comprised of ceramides and hyaluronic acid. that leads to skin cancer.

Melanin Diet

Melanin People referred to as Sun people, should eat foods rich in vitamin C–rich such as berries, leafy green vegetables, and citrus, to optimize melanin production. We should take a regular supplement of vitamin C also.

Melanin protects the hair color, skin, and eyes from sunlight damage and other sources of electromagnetic radiation sources. Humans with blonde and naturally red hair will require serious Sun blocking protection to avoid skin cancer. We become depressed, suicidal, and vitamin D deficient, experiencing lowered immune functioning when deprived of sunlight. People lacking melanin experience malfunctioning to the nervous system. The Sun helps to strengthen us, then our melanin won't allow energy to escape. There are many missing Sun people because evil hue-mans are pulling melanin for adrenaline. The Sun people have black hole properties. We are despised because we are the people with the God particles.

Melanin Takeaway: *Celebrate our heritage; our melanin is more valuable than Gold. It's magic.*

Notes

Reality

Reality is transtemporal, which means transcending time the influence or communication between one time and another.

Reality is the act of what we are experiencing, yet it doesn't necessarily have to be the truth. Truth is acceptable information making it conditionally accurate.

Our reality is being directed by others. Our adapted language is a spell referred to us as spelling words. Our most frequently used greeting is hello and good-bye.

The Earth orbits around the Sun takes 365 days.

Reality Takeaway: *We are co-creator of our reality.*

Time

The time is conversion previously was ten months. Now, its 12 months. Any person who can control our time control us; Chronos time is the quantity of time in seconds, minutes to hours. Besides, Kairos time is the quality of time given at the right opportune moment.

Time Takeaway: We must be *more cautiously mindful of our energies. We should heavily focus on* celebrating the full moon, stars and seasons compared to man-made holidays.

Tidal Gauges
When there is a low tide, the water isn't being pulled anywhere remains still; the water is concentrated to the part of Earth wherever gravity is closest to it.

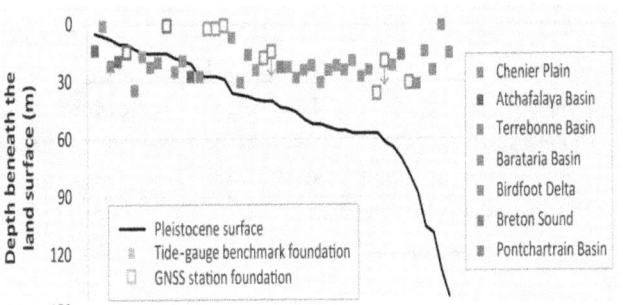

This Photo by Unknown Author is licensed under CC BY

HOLIDAYS (man-made)

A solstice and an equinox are sort of opposites. The two solstices happen in June (20 or 21) and December (21 or 22).

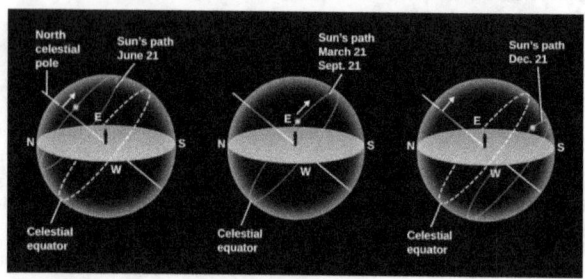

This Photo by Unknown Author is licensed under CC BY

These are the days when the Sun's path in the sky is the farthest north or south from the Equator. There is a man-made holiday placed around the solstice and equinox based on the volume of celebratory energy. The holidays and the Gregorian calendar only account for the solar calendar, excluding the lunar calendar. Holidays and Time are both constructs. The lunar calendar informs us of the appearance of the Moon every 15 days and a new Moon in 30 days. Based on our planetary energies, the actual **New year is March 21st.** The Chinese, Persian, and Iranian celebrates the new year in March.

THE ARRIVAL

We have traveled many years to get here! Now what?

(Our divine light starts to dimmer over a lifespan.)
At the beginning of a human life, the genetic code converts in chromosome 23 from each parent. The genes justified the being of a human what type of person we will become to instruct on how to grow.

Let's walk through the process of a newborn baby.

Melanin sperm journeys inside of a vagina, speeding towards the egg carrying genetic code. The embryo resides inside the placenta possessing eyes of pure Melanin and stem cells. Within nine months, it resides in a calm, peaceful sanctuary. During birth, the gender is determined by the father's sperm: female X or male Y, then newborn placed directly on a stranger's chest snuggled by warm blankets for the first hour of life. Then staff takes it away from bonding time to probe and run PKU screening and determine the weight, length then inject vitamin K into the infant. Forced into a noisy world, the infant adapts to recognize their mother's voice, dream, and display of emotions. Over time, our environment, parents, caretakers, family, and friends will play a pivotal in our outcome. We were programmed to believe a female or male's traits by learning specific feminine and masculine characteristics. **Gender** is used to separate behavioral patterns. We learn a man should protect the woman as she unconditionally loves and supports him.

The Arrival Takeaway: *Our environment, our parents, friends, caretakers will be pivotal in how our future will become.*

BELONGING

The sense of family is uplifting because there lies a yearning to determine to find an affinity for a place or situation. We desire to be a part of a greater purpose than ourselves. Humans long to be interconnected to family, friends, community, and to the universe.

The phenomena of celestial objects such as asteroids, planets, Moons, star clusters, nebulae, and galaxies exist as evidence to evolutionary lifeforce. The universe's evolution has always been intriguing to most people. Electromagnetic radiation is the spectrum to forms of energies where our ancestral journey begins. This spectrum of light is the reflection our ancestors used as a guide in a dark world to track time by their observations in the skies. The movement of the different objects was tied to religious rituals.

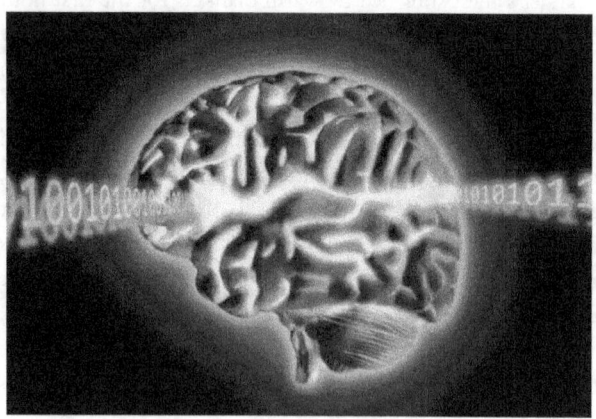

This Photo by Unknown Author is licensed under CC BY

Meditation - it is when we are entering our spiritual point connecting ourselves with everything else is around us.

- yoga.
- meditation.
- taking certain supplements.
- doing a detox or cleanse.
- using crystals

What blocks the third eye?

Our third eye potentially can block our ability to concentrate and interpret the signs all around us. It can be prevented through a healing process. Blockages occur from fear, karma, jealousy, hate, greed, self-doubt, disappointments, lack of self-love, gossiping, and this list goes on to assess injuries where bone fracture is suspected.

Worrying about the future creates a chain of negative energy in our life. To create an abundant future, we must first believe the future we want is waiting for us.

When we meditate on a bad future, we are creating the end we don't want. The universe delivers what we ruminate upon; so, stop thinking about things that will lower our frequency. Ensure we are focusing our energy on a quality one, and that will, in turn, boost our frequency now.

How can we open our third eye quickly?

How do we stimulate our pineal gland?
The following 8 tips can help!

Pay attention to our dreams. ...
Focus our meditation on our third eye. ...
Practice breath work. ...
Practice Kundalini yoga. ...
Don't give up on regular yoga practice either. ...
Eat a nutritious diet. ...
Start using essential oils. ...
Meditate with crystals...

Removing erosion calcification

Calcification occurs when calcium grows in muscle, arteries, or organs and disturb our body's normal processes. Transported through the bloodstream, the deposits can interrupt vital processes in the brain and heart. Chlorella is a single-celled green alga that goes on the attack against heavy metals, increases blood oxygen, and repairs damaged tissues.

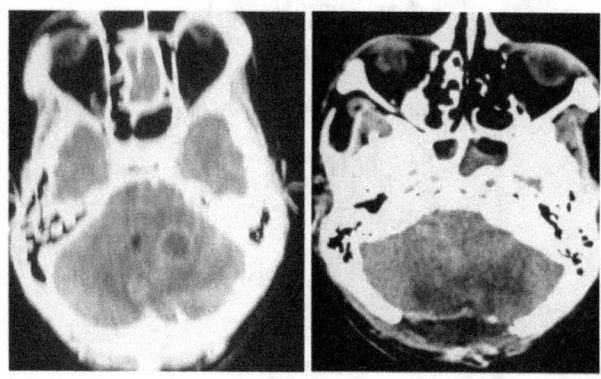

This Photo by Unknown Author is licensed under CC BY

Soul You, Vol. I: The Grand Awakening

What if I 'activate' my pineal gland?

Our pineal gland is a small, soybean-sized gland located in the brain inside of the adreno-gland. This produces melatonin, which is a hormone that helps regulate sleep and wakefulness. After the Vietnam war, the late 60s early 70s, whenever a soldier dies, there is an Autopsy. These were performed on 75-80% African American Vietnam black soldiers who had a large pineal gland organ complex molecule antioxidant.

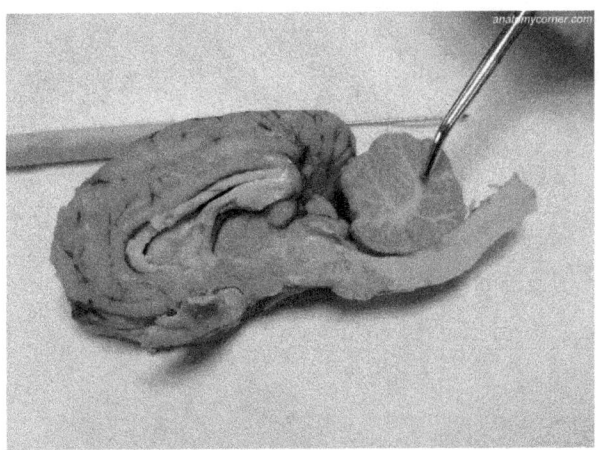

This Photo by Unknown Author is licensed under CC BY-

Notes

_____

_____

_____

_____

_____

_____

_____

_____

_____

References

Tracking dates for winter and summer

solstice info visit: https://www.usno.navy.mil/USNO

equinox info visit:
https://www.nationalgeographic.org/encyclopedia/equinox

Climate:
https://www.ipcc.ch/

Egyptian Culture:
https://www.anciaent.eu/Egyptian_Culture/

Leave a review and purchase other books directly on

WWW.SHERIKADUNCAN.COM

THE SETUP NOVEL

SOUL YOU BOOK COLLECTION
Soul You Vol I: The Grand Awakening
Soul You Vol. II: The Procreator
Soul You Vol III: The Protector
Soul You Vol. IV: Scribble Journal

media@sherikaduncan.com
www.instagram.com/sherika.duncan
www.twitter.com/sherikaduncan_
www.facebook.com/sherikaduncanauthor

Copyright © 2021 Sherika Duncan Enterprise

All rights reserved.

www.ingramcontent.com/pod-product-compliance
Lightning Source LLC
Chambersburg PA
CBHW062205100526
44589CB00014B/1960